Adobe's Photoshop Elements 14 - What's New?

A Guide to New Features for Elements Users

by

Beverly Richards Schulz

Eric Johnson

Published by:

Instructional & Photographic Services

www.BevSchulz.com

Adobe's Photoshop Elements 14 – What's New?

Publication Date – December 15, 2015

Published by Instructional & Photographic Services

Cover Design: Beverly Richards Schulz and Eric Johnson

TABLE OF CONTENTS

Introduction

About the Cover...i

Online Courses in Digital Photography...iii

Why What's New? v

How to Use this Book vii

Getting Photos to Use for the Exercises ix

Questions? We're Listening!...xi

Mac Users xiii

Getting Started

Using the Welcome Screen 1

Application Options..4

Interactive Features 5

Create A New Catalog Message 7

New and Improved Editing Features

Easy File Sizing 9

Haze Removal 15

Straighten Tool Enhancements 23

Speed Effect 31

Shake Reduction 43

Refine Selection Brush Improvements 55

Smart Looks.. 65

Photomerge° Changes 75

Elements 14 Organizer

People Recognition 84

Date and Time 85

Places 86

Importing 87

Tidbits

Organizer Catalog Message 90

Guided Edit Redesign 92

Guided Edit Previews 94

Changes to Preferences 95

Resetting Preferences 97

Changes to File Info 99

Appendix

The Cover Image 101

About the Authors.. 113

INTRODUCTION

ABOUT THE COVER

Our cover image showcases a few of Elements 14's new and old features, in particular Haze Removal as well as the Refine Selection options and the Out of Bounds Guided Edit. We also used the Noise filter, lots of selection tools, the gradient tool, layer masks, and some spot-specific saturating of colors. We'll leave the exact details, as they say in old college textbooks, "…as an exercise for the student", but if you're interested in a general workflow, see the appendix at the back of the book for a few ideas to get you started. Make it your own way!

ONLINE COURSES IN DIGITAL PHOTOGRAPHY

The genesis of this book really came from our experience teaching online courses in Photography and digital photo editing tools such as Adobe Photoshop, Photoshop Elements, and Photoshop Lightroom. We've been teaching online courses in photography and digital editing since the early 2000's and have had more than 70,000 students take our courses. This book is an outgrowth of that experience and our passion for teaching photography.

We teach online courses through Ed2go (www.ed2go.com) and they are available through over 2,500 partner colleges, universities, and educational organizations in the United States, Canada, Australia, and other places worldwide. You can see a list of all our courses and find a local school offering them via this link:

www.bevschulz.com

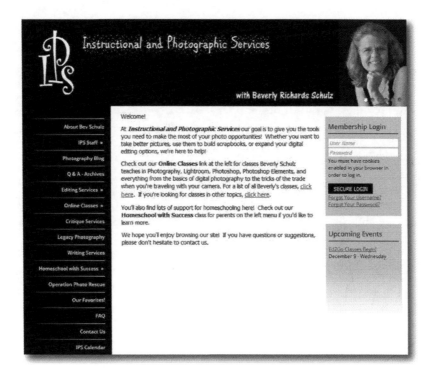

Classes Offered

We offer six-week online courses in the following subjects:

- ✧ **Discover Digital Photography** is a broad, general overview of digital photography.

- ✧ **Secrets of Better Photography** is a nuts-and-bolts course on how to use your camera, settings, composition, exposure—a general "how to be a better photographer" course. Want to master your camera? This is the class.

- ✧ **Travel Photography for the Digital Photographer** is a class on putting your camera to work in a wide variety of locations and photographic situations.

- ✧ **Introduction to Lightroom** is an overview of Adobe's Lightroom tool, one of our favorite photo editing, management, and presentation tools.

- ✧ **Photoshop Elements for the Digital Photographer (Parts 1 and 2)** is a thorough set of courses on Adobe's extremely popular editing program Photoshop Elements 13. Designed for those that don't need the full version of Photoshop (or its expense) and what we recommend for many photographers. This class is designed specifically around the needs of digital photographers.

- ✧ **Photoshop for the Digital Photographer (Parts 1 and 2)**, is our class for the granddaddy of photo editors. Although Photoshop is used by graphic artists and designers, in these classes we concentrate on the tools for photographers.

- ✧ **Digital Scrapbooking (with Photoshop Elements)** uses Photoshop Elements and focuses on scrapbooking and similar projects. This is a great follow up to Elements Parts 1 and 2!

- ✧ **Homeschool with Success!** This isn't a photography class, but is for those interested in homeschooling their children. (Beverly homeschooled her son through high school graduation and is excited to share her experiences with other homeschoolers.)

WHY "WHAT'S NEW?"

We're so glad you picked up this book! A typical book on new software covers how to use everything, but you won't find all that information here. Instead, we wrote a quick guide for users upgrading from a previous version of Photoshop Elements (think of it as weekend class on what's new!) and included a number of features we think you'll appreciate. Even if Photoshop Elements still has areas you haven't explored, don't worry! We don't expect expert knowledge—we'll walk you through each step of the way.

Browsing available books on Photoshop Elements might lead you to the conclusion that plenty of authors have already written books on the subject. We ourselves have been teaching online courses in Photoshop Elements for over 10 years. Why another book?

This book outlines the key changes from Photoshop Elements 13 to Photoshop Elements 14 and you'll see how to put those new features to work without having to sift through information you already know. We've focused on changes in Photoshop Elements Editor for the majority of the book, but you'll also see what's new in Organizer, although most of that is an update to existing features and you'll find it quick and easy to use.

The genesis of this book came as we considered our options for teaching Photoshop Elements 14. For years, we've had students who knew the previous version and wanted to know what was new, what changed, and how to use the new features without having to dig information out of help files, reviews, and spend a lot of time on experimentation. We hope this book will enable previous Elements user to get the most out of Photoshop Elements 14 in the shortest amount of time. It's great software—let's get started!

HOW TO USE THIS BOOK

Each section of this book covers a different topic. You can work through them in the order we've presented them or jump around to find what interests you. Each topic is independent in its content, unless it ties into another new feature of Photoshop Elements 14.

At the beginning of each section, you'll see a quick overview of the new feature, its location in the software, and steps for using it. Following that, you'll see a more in-depth discussion of how it works, what it's for, and a discussion of other Photoshop Elements features that are related, including alternatives you might use if you need more control or options to achieve a certain effect.

For most topics, we've provided images at our download site so you can work with the same image we use in the book. You can download all the images at once or one at time, as you need them. You'll find detailed directions on downloading coming up next!

Prerequisites: What you need to know

Since this is a book on what's new, not a complete guide to Photoshop Elements, we've written it using the following assumptions:

- ✦ Your computer meets Adobe's requirements for running Photoshop Elements 14.
- ✦ You have access to Adobe's Photoshop Elements 14, installed and working, on your Windows or Mac computer.
- ✦ You have previous knowledge of Adobe's Photoshop Elements or Adobe Photoshop.
- ✦ You have Internet access to download images and access our forums if you need help.
- ✦ You're comfortable downloading images, creating folders, saving files, and opening and closing Photoshop Elements.

GETTING PHOTOS TO USE FOR THE EXERCISES

You'll find the images for the exercises in this book online at:

http://ips.smugmug.com/PSE-14-Whats-New/PSE-14-Download-Images/n-qvfMMF

Once you arrive at the page, you'll have several options for downloading images.

Option 1: If you're comfortable with entering your email address, downloading a Zip file, and then extracting the images from there, click DOWNLOAD ALL and follow the directions. You'll receive an email with a link that will download a Zip file and then you'll extract it on your computer before you use the images.

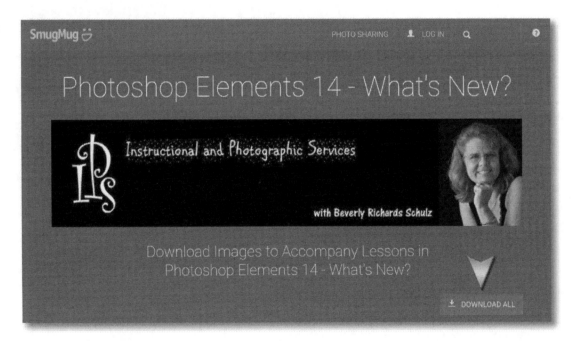

On most computers, the easiest way to extract files from a zip folder is to double-click the zipped folder and then drag the images out into another folder.

Very important: Elements *cannot* read images from a zip folder so they *must* be extracted!

Eyes glazing over? Doesn't sound like fun? There's another way!

Option 2: To download one image at a time, go to http://ips.smugmug.com/PSE-14-Whats-New/PSE-14-Download-Images/n-qvfMMF and find the image you want to download. In the lower-right corner of that image, you'll see a down arrow. Click the down arrow and that one image will download to your computer into your Downloads folder. From there, you can open it in Photoshop Elements, or move it to a folder on your Desktop (or wherever you want it) and then use it from there.

Still having trouble? Contact us through www.BevSchulz.com and we can help!

QUESTIONS? WE'RE LISTENING!

First and foremost, we are teachers... If you have a question, you're welcome to join our forum and post questions where you'll get answers!

Go **to** www.BevSchulz.com and contact us.

MAC USERS

What You Need to Know

As Photoshop Elements evolved over the years, the Windows and Mac versions of Photoshop Elements have become more and more consistent. Today they are very similar, if not identical, in function and appearance in most respects.

Because of this similarity (and the fact that Windows users make up a significant majority of computer users worldwide) we'll use the Windows version in our examples. However, we will call out any relevant differences, such as keystrokes, substantial changes in how features look or work, and so on, so you'll find this book equally useful. If you've taken any of our online courses, you're familiar with this approach and that it works well.

We'll assume, however, you're comfortable with the basics of working on the Mac, creating folders, using applications, navigating through folders and directories, using a web browser to download images, moving files from one folder to another, and so on. This isn't a course on how to use your Mac (or your Windows machine) but rather how to use Elements on your computer, whatever operating system you're using.

Where there are major differences, we'll be sure to call those out. No worries!

GETTING STARTED

Photoshop Elements is two (possibly three) programs packaged together. You have the ability to customize how Elements launches, what program runs first, as well as some other options that have changed in version 14.

NEW WELCOME SCREEN

The first thing you'll see when you launch Photoshop Elements 14 is a new Welcome screen. You'll see that it changes a lot and includes animation. Yours may not match what you see here and that's normal. Adobe changes what it shows from time to time. The Welcome screen does let you customize how you start and work with Elements so it's worth taking a look.

Using the Welcome Screen

If you launch Elements, you may see it automatically:

If Elements doesn't open to this automatically, you can view it any time by choosing Help > Welcome from either the Photo Editor or Organizer. To customize the behavior of the Welcome screen, click the Gear icon in the top-right corner.

Use the On Start Always Launch: menu to choose what you want Elements to do when you first launch it:

- ✧ **Welcome Screen** will always bring up this Welcome screen first.
- ✧ **Photo Editor** will take you directly to the Photo Editor without showing you this Welcome screen.
- ✧ **Organizer w**ill open the Organizer without showing the Welcome Screen.

Note: *These changes will take place next time you launch Elements, so choosing Photo Editor from the On Start Always Launch menu won't launch the Editor immediately.*

Personally we prefer to set this to Photo Editor (as that's where we do most of our work), but if you work more in Organizer, you may want to choose that. Or you can go to the Welcome screen and choose each time you enter Photoshop Elements.

Application Options

At the bottom of the Welcome screen are options for how to launch the Editor, Organizer, or Video editor.

If you click the Photo Editor button, Elements will launch Photo Editor directly. However, if you click the arrow to the right of the Photo Editor button, you'll have some options:

⟡ **Photo Editor:** You can choose to reopen a list of recently used images, open a new image, or start with a blank file.

⟡ **Organizer.** You have no options here—just click the button and Organizer launches.

⟡ **Video Editor.** If you have Premiere Elements (Adobe's video editing package) installed on your computer, you can open it here. Adobe offers Premiere Elements bundled together with

Photoshop Elements. If you don't have Premiere, this choice gives you an option to download it as a free trial. We won't be covering Premiere Elements in this book.

After making your choice, click Done to set the change for next time you start or Cancel if you want to leave the On Start Always Launch setting as it was.

Interactive Features

Let's look at one last feature before we leave the Welcome screen. Inside the Welcome Screen box and above the buttons you may find some links you can click. These may change over time so what you see here may not be what you're seeing on your screen.

For example, in the above image of the Welcome screen, you can click an option to Explore more Elements 14 features (which takes you to Adobe's web site for a page showing new Elements features), an option to browse some online Video Tutorials, and a link to Adobe's Facebook page to Join the conversation.

And, of course, you can close the Welcome screen by clicking the **X** in the upper-right corner.

CREATE A NEW CATALOG MESSAGE

If you're using Elements 14 and trying to save an image, you may encounter this message and it can be a bit confusing!

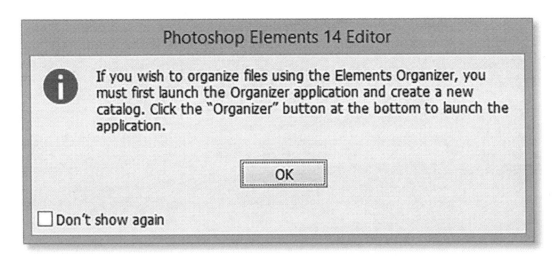

Adobe is letting you know that if you want the file you're saving to be available in Organizer, you haven't yet created an Organizer catalog, and therefore, you can't have that image in the (non-existent) catalog. So . . . .

You have two choices here:

1. If you're not using Organizer (now or later) and just want to get rid of the message forever,

    a. Check the Don't show again box.

    b. Click OK.

2. Or, if you do want to use Organizer later, just click OK and once you've set up your Organizer catalog, you can go back and add this image and any others you need to.

See more details on this feature in the Tidbits section at the end of this book.

NEW AND IMPROVED EDITING FEATURES

EASY FILE SIZING

Resizing images for a specific purpose is a frequent task for any photo editor. Photoshop Elements 14 has a new **Guided** feature to help simplify this process called Resize Your Photo.

To use this feature, open any image you'd like to resize. We'll use *Haystacks* from the set of download images (see information in the Introduction of this book on downloading images) but any image is fine. Once the image is open, click Guided at the top of the Elements workspace, then open the Basics section just below that.

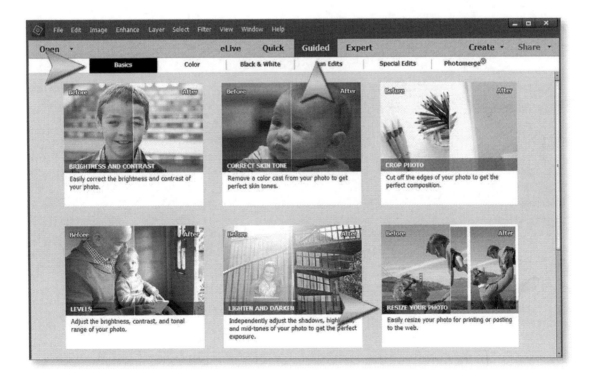

With the Guided > Basics options visible, click Resize your Photo.

Typical of **Guided** edits, Adobe lists each step on the right side of the screen.

Your first step lets you indicate whether you're going to use this image on the Web (for a website, email, Facebook or Pinterest posting, and so on.) or for printing. The difference between choosing Web and Print is how you describe the size. With Web, you'll specify the size in pixels or bytes. With Print, you'll specify the size in inches or centimeters. We'll walk through both.

If you choose Web as the output, you'll have the following options for step 2. Click the menu and you'll see these options:

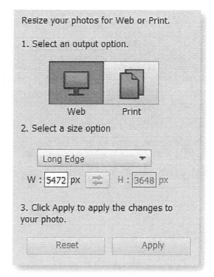

✦ **Long Edge** requires you to enter the size the longest edge (H: for height or W: for width) should be. Elements will automatically adjust the other side to match the aspect ratio (original shape).

- ✧ **Short Edge** lets you enter the size the shortest side (H: for height or W: for width) should be, and Elements will automatically adjust the other side to match the aspect ratio.

- ✧ **Width and Height** lets you enter both width and height. A crop frame will appear over the image showing what portions of the image will be kept. You can use the mouse to click and drag this crop frame over the image to choose what part of the image to keep.

- ✧ **File Size** allows you to enter the maximum size for the image.

A little practice is in order to see how this works. Using Haystacks as a sample, we'll resize it for an email under several different scenarios.

Resizing for Web

Let's assume you need an online image that is no larger than 800 pixels in either dimension.

1. Choose Web.

2. Choose Long Edge and enter 800 for W(idth).

3. Click Apply. This will set the changes.

4. Click the arrow above Next below Step 3 to indicate what to do with the resulting image.

You'll have three general choices:

- Save the image to your computer

- Continue working with the resized image either in **Quick** or **Expert** mode

- Post the resized images online to the listed options

- ❖ If you choose to save, you'll be presented with the typical Save or Save As dialog (as you normally would via File > Save or Save As) and you can save the image. It will also resize the image you currently have in the editor.
- ❖ If you choose either In Quick or in **Expert** in the Continue Editing section, Elements will leave **Guided** and go to **Quick** or **Expert** and show you the resized image.
- ❖ Choosing one of the Share options will let you upload your resized image online through the service you choose. Note that the available services may change as Adobe updates Elements.

Click the Done checkmark in the lower-right corner when you've finished and return to the Basics view under **Guided**.

Resizing for Print

Now let's assume you want to print the image as a 4 x 6-inch print, regardless of whether or not the image happens to be vertically or horizontally oriented. Print sizing is a little different from sizing for the Web in that you need to determine the physical size you want the print as well as the *resolution* of the print measured in pixels per inch (PPI).

Normally for good-quality prints you want a resolution of 200 to 300 PPI. Guided > Resize Your Photo resizes using the currently chosen resolution for the image—but unfortunately you can't change that in the Guided area. This is really important to know before resizing! If the image is currently using a resolution of 72 PPI to calculate the size, that's the resolution you'll end up with after resizing. 72

PPI will print very poorly. So before using Guided > Resize Your Photo, it's wise to verify that the resolution is set as you want it. Easy to do but you'll need to leave the Guided area to do it.

Checking the Print Resolution

To check (and change) the resolution of an image, choose **Expert**, then Image > Resize > Image Size.

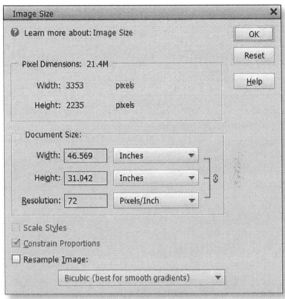

The Image Size window tells you the Pixel Dimensions of the image as well as the Document Size at the currently chosen resolution. You want a Resolution of 300 for a good quality print.

As you can see from the example at the right, with the Resolution to set 72 Pixels/Inch (PPI) it produces a very large image—it's 46 inches wide! 300 PPI would be a much better choice for a quality print.

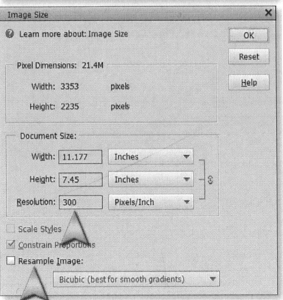

To use 300 PPI as the resolution for sizing for the image, in Image > Resize > Image Size make sure the Resample Image box is unchecked (otherwise it will resize the image for you instead of recalculating the size), enter the new resolution of 300, and see the recalculated size.

Once that's done you can use the **Guided** area to resize. Here are the steps to follow:

- ✧ In Step 1, choose Print.
- ✧ In Step 2, choose Long Edge and enter 6 (inches) for W(idth).
- ✧ Click Apply. This will set the changes.
- ✧ Now click Next below Step 3 to choose what you want to do with the resulting image.

As with the Web option, you'll be able to save the image or work with it in **Expert** or **Quick** editing. You'll also have the option to print it. What you won't have is the option to upload it to a sharing site, which makes sense since you've sized this for printing, not online use.

Click the Done checkmark in the lower-right corner when you're done to return to the Basics view in the **Guided** area.

To Use Guided Resize . . . or Not

We find this feature handy for quickly resizing images, particularly for the Web. For printing . . . . if the resolution is already set, it's fine. Otherwise, it may be just as easy to resize in the Image > Resize > Image Size window or use the Crop tool and set the size there. As with many things in Elements, there are often various ways to reach the same goal and the best one is the one that's easiest for you!

HAZE REMOVAL

What does Haze Removal do?

Haze can come from any number of sources: pollution or particles in the air, strong light creating overexposure in shadows, a lightly fogged up lens (or shooting through a window), underwater photos, and so on. Regardless of how it got there, students often ask how to get rid of it. Elements 14 added a Haze Reduction feature and it gets our vote for the handiest new editing feature in Elements 14.

To use Haze Reduction choose **Expert** in Elements. We'll use Ocelot from the download set but feel free to use any image you like. (Thanks to Mickela Schulz for letting us use her photo!)

We can improve this great photo by working with contrast—darks aren't as dark as they should be and due to shooting through glass, the image looks a bit washed out.

Choose Enhance > Haze Removal and the Haze Removal window will appear.

You can see there is already adjustment applied immediately as you use the Haze Removal tool. These are the default settings and they may or may not be ideal so let's see how to adjust them.

The controls are simple:

✦ Adjust the Haze Reduction slider back and forth to control the amount of haze reduction. Pushed all the way to the left you'll see virtually no adjustment. Pushing it all the way to the right it will apply the most reduction it can.

✦ The Sensitivity slider is a little more subtle. It controls what is and what isn't considered *haze* in the image.

✦ The Before and After toggle lets you switch back and forth between the unedited and edited versions.

In the preceding image, we adjusted both Haze Reduction and Sensitivity to what looked better (there's no particular formula for this—you choose what looks better to you!) The beauty of this feature is that it can very quickly fix a hazy image. Toggling back and forth between Before and After can help you see details that may be getting washed out.

When you're done, click OK or you can click Cancel if you want to cancel the changes you've made in the Haze Removal window.

One thing to be cautious of is over-processing the image. If you increase the contrast too much you can make the image look artificial or like digital editing has been used a bit too much! It's okay for the image to have lots of contrast and have lots of visual pop but apply too much and it looks artificial. For example, in the following image, we used Haze Removal to remove much of the haze but it left the image grainy and with too much contrast that doesn't quite look natural. The background is too dark, the grass has too much contrast, and the fog doesn't look quite natural. Go for a balance! Better to remove some of the problem than all of it and introduce a worse problem.

Tech Stuff: Haze and Haze Removal

Haze can be caused by a number of things, but from an editing point of view it's usually caused by two things:

✦ Insufficient contrast causing the image to look washed out and less distinct. If it's not too severe this is relatively easy to fix in Elements by increasing the contrast correctly.

✧ Interference between the camera and the subject, typically in the form of mist, particles in the air, and so on. This is a tougher one to fix as the information about the image itself is being partially blocked. Contrast you can fix. Missing detail... not really.

One of the first things we do when editing an image that doesn't look right is to check the image's histogram. The histogram shows how the tones in the image are distributed. You can view the histogram for any image in Elements by choosing Window > Histogram.

Here is the histogram for the unedited Ocelot image:

The histogram shows tones from black to white across the chart. Notice that for the first part of the histogram (blacks) is empty. There are no black or dark black tones in this image. An ocelot has black fur so that's probably a problem! Generally, a gap here implies a lack of contrast. Here's how *Ocelot's* histogram looks after Haze Removal:

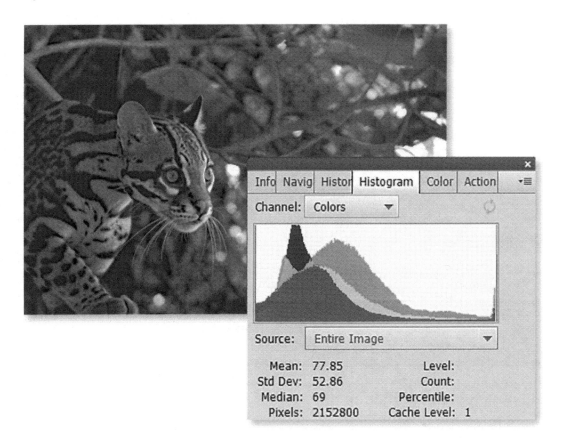

Note that the histogram spreads out quite a bit more and has tones in the black and deep shadow areas of the histogram.

There is no *right* histogram for all photos, but a histogram can be very helpful in evaluating the distribution of tones in the image.

As you might have guessed, Haze Removal essentially adjusts contrast. Elements has several features for adjusting contrast and you could use them on an image like this as well. Could you get similar results without the Haze Removal features? Sure. Prior to this feature the way we would have done it would be to use Enhance > Adjust Lighting > Levels.

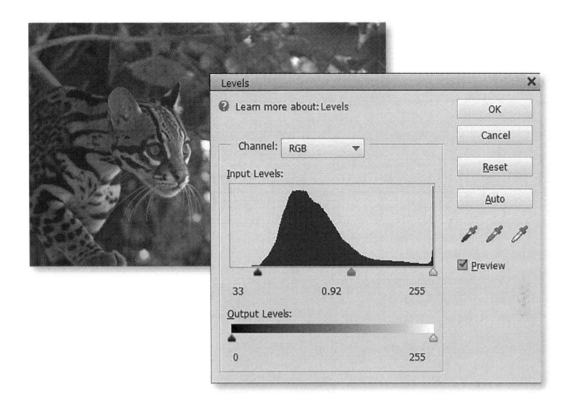

Here again we see the histogram (it's important!). We moved the black slider at the left in to the beginning of the mountain of the histogram to indicate where black tones should start. We moved the midtone slider (gray arrow in the middle) slightly to the right to darken midtones just a bit, which also helped with contrast. We left the white slider at the far right alone. Be sure to watch the image as you adjust the sliders. The histogram is a guide—not the rule. Results are what matter!

You could also use Enhance > Adjust Lighting > Brightness/Contrast and adjust the Contrast. Levels is more flexible in that it controls the blacks, midtones, and whites separately so it's often preferred for best quality.

STRAIGHTEN TOOL ENHANCEMENTS

What Does It Do?

Along with cropping, straightening an image is a common correction. Since the early days of Photoshop Elements, the Straighten tool let us draw a horizontal guideline and Elements aligned the image. But aligning based on a vertical line was a bit trickier—if you didn't know to hold the CTRL key down (Mac users: Command key), drawing a vertical line resulted in rotating the image nearly 90 degrees as Elements took that vertical line to be the horizon! Some creative types found a workaround by rotating the image 90 degrees, then straightening, then rotating it back 90 degrees.

With Photoshop Elements 14, things got easier! The Straighten tool is more intelligent now and will choose to rotate horizontally or vertically depending on the line you draw. We'll use *Danger Sign* from the download set to demonstrate, but of course feel free to use any image you like.

Where Do I Find it?

With the image open in Elements, choose **Expert** and then the Straighten tool which is in the Modify section of the Tool Box. (By the way, have you ever wondered what that icon *is?* It's a carpenter's level!)

How Can I Use it?

For this tool, you'll want to have the Options bar visible. If it isn't, click Tool Options at the bottom of the screen. These options are very helpful in determining what the final outcome of your rotation will be because as an image rotates the corners rotate and you'll have to decide what to do about that. You can re-crop or remove them, but that's a little abstract, so let's take a look at that visually.

Below you see Danger Sign with a frame around it indicating the original outlines of the image. In the second image, Danger Sign has been rotated counter-clockwise but the frame indicating the original size is left in place. You can see how parts of the image are rotated out of the frame (and how blank triangles show up) when an image is rotated. The Straighten tool's options let you decide what you're going to do with those triangles.

The first option is Grow or Shrink. Grow or Shrink will adjust the size of the image to include blank space. It uses the Background color from the Background color swatch in the Tool Box. Use this option when you want to keep all of the image

after it's rotated. This will change the dimensions of the image, usually making it a little bigger.

The second option is Remove Background. This crops out all the triangles that rotated out of the frame or were created inside the frame. It will shrink the image a bit as it crops away the triangles to make the image rectangular. You'll probably use this option if you're printing since it gives you a clean edge.

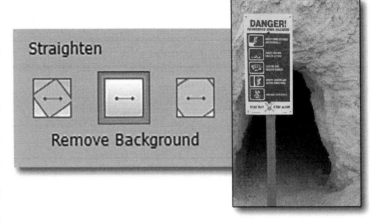

The last of the three options is Original Size. This keeps the rotated image exactly the same size as it was before. It's as if the frame was locked and the image rotate within the frame and the outside triangles were clipped away. However, the inside triangles will remain and will be filled with the

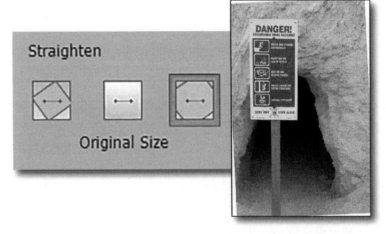

Background color from the Background color swatch in the Tool Box.

The two other checkboxes in the Options bar are as follows:

- ✧ **Rotate All Layers.** If you're working with a multi-layer image, all the layers are straightened. Uncheck this box if you only want to straighten the current layer, leaving the others unchanged.

- ✧ **Autofill Edges.** Elements will attempt to fill in the empty spaces caused by rotating inside and outside of the frame with fill to match the image. Depending on the image, this can work quite well, particularly in an image like Danger Sign where the edges are non-specific patterns like rocks. Something more detailed, like tree branches, a person or a car, probably won't fill very well but you can give it a try. This option will only be available if Grow or Shrink or Original Size is chosen. Since Remove Background crops everything away, there's nothing to fill so this checkbox will be gray if Remove Background is chosen.

In the two images above you see how Autofill worked on Danger Sign. The first image is done with Grow or Shrink and the second used Original Size. If you look closely you can see some flaws (particularly on the right image at the right edge it looks a bit artifical or poorly cloned), but in general it did a pretty good job!

That won't always be the case. In the following image notice how after rotating the image so our young snorkeler is standing straight and the horizon is flat, Autofill filled in some areas that don't match and look slightly bizarre.

Using it's very simple: click and drag a line that *should* be horizontal or vertical, then release the mouse button. Elements will rotate the image so the line you drew becomes horizontal or vertical. If the line is closer to flat than vertical (less than 45 degrees), it will rotate to make the line horizontal. If it's closer to vertical than flat (greater than 45 degrees), it will orient the image vertically. Simple! Being able to do this vertically more easily is a nice improvement.

By the way, this tool is also available in **Quick** editing and you can also orient vertically there now as well. Quick editing allows you to see a before and after on the screen side by side if you like but doesn't give the option to Grow or Shrink, leaving the triangles blank and the whole image intact. Three options are available:

- ✧ **Autofill Edges.** This works just like it does in **Expert** and Autofill fills in the empty space caused by rotating.

- ✧ **Maintain Canvas Size.** This keeps the image the size of the canvas, or the whole image from corner to corner. As the image rotates, blank areas will be filled in or not, depending on whether or not you chose Autofill, which is essentially the same option as Original Size in **Expert**.

- ✧ **Maintain Image Size.** This expands the image to include blank space triangles so none of the image is lost. Essentially, this is the same option as Grow or Shrink. Blank areas will be filled in if Autofill Edges is checked.

Let Me Try

Danger Sign would look more balanced if the sign were straight up and down. Here's what we did to straighten it. Feel free to try this using your own image if you like!

1. Choose **Expert** and open Danger Sign (File > Open).

2. Choose the Straighten tool, located at the bottom of the Tool box in the Modify section.

3. Choose Remove Background in the Options bar.

4. Move the mouse pointer to the top-right corner of the sign and click and drag down so the line drawn is exactly

along the right, vertical edge of the sign. Drawing past the end helped us get it as accurate as possible.

5. Release the mouse when you have the line perfectly aligned.

After releasing the mouse Elements rotates the image so the edge of the sign is vertical. Didn't get it quite right? No worries. Use Edit > Undo and give it another try. Particularly with objects with some perspective, you may need to experiment to find the right line to properly balance the image. Usually something towards the center works best.

Tips on straightening

It's often easier to get straightening to look right if you work with a horizontal line instead of a vertical one. Vertical objects, however, tend to have strong perspective to them and if you rotate an image without taking perspective into account it may throw off the rest of the image.

In the following image we clearly see perspective in the towering landscape of New York City. We might be tempted to straighten the image so that the buildings are perfectly straight. The results aren't pretty!

29

Original   Flagpole   Building in left background

Perspective is part of the normal view of things. When straightening vertically, try to pick something in the middle of the image that's not as affected by perspective. Even something as close as the flagpole in the middle image gives the image a bit of a skewed look, and straightening based on the building in the back left really distorts things. The truth is, this image is probably fine like it was! The perspective is natural and our real subject—the girl in the foreground, looks vertically correct.

We also find it helpful to draw as long a line as possible when straightening.

SPEED EFFECT

What Does It Do?

Speed Effect is a new Guided feature in Elements 14. It gives the illusion of rapid movement to an otherwise static image. This is a fun one, especially with images of children.

Where Do I Find it?

When you're in Photoshop Elements, choose **Guided** at the top of the Elements workspace. In the bar directly below, choose Fun Edits.

Click the Speed Effects thumbnail and you'll see the Speed Effects panel open at the right.

How Do I Use it?

Guided features come with a complete list of instructions in the guide area on the right side of the screen—it doesn't get much easier than that! To add the speed effect once you're in Guided:

- ✧ Select the area of the image you want to look like it's moving
- ✧ Apply the effect
- ✧ Fine tune the amount of speed you want
- ✧ Fine tune the area it covers

And you're done!

Let Me Try!

Let's walk through an example. We'll use Mowing from the downloads.

It would be fun to make this image seem like he's going as fast as he probably thinks he is. The Speed effect is perfect for this. Follow these steps to add the effect.

1. With Mowing open in the Elements Photo Editor, choose **Guided**.

2. Choose Fun Edits from the bar below and then click the Speed Effect thumbnail.

3. In Step 1, click Quick Selection Tool. Adjust your brush size to a size large enough to paint easily. We chose a size of about 60 pixels although the exact number isn't important. Paint with your cursor until you've selected the entire mower. Use different size brushes if needed. Make sure you don't leave any holes in the selection. Remember, this doesn't need to be perfect, just generally selected.

4. Use Subtract to clean up any stray areas you don't want selected. When you're done, your selection might look like this:

5. In Step 2, click Add Speed Effect. This is going to blur out the majority of the area selected with a motion blur. Adjust the direction of the speed blur by clicking and dragging the Angle control and you can adjust how strong you like it. We added a couple clicks of Increase but it's entirely up to you! It's okay if it looks like it's too much! You'll adjust that in a minute.

6. In Step 3, click Add Focus Area. Your mouse pointer will turn to a crosshair. Click and drag lines in the direction of the blur to erase areas of the effect. For example, we clicked from the far left to the right numerous times erasing the blur effect in front and on the front of the tractor and boy.

3. Click the Add Focus Area button and then click and drag over the area where you would like to remove the effect.

Add Focus Area

7. We're getting there! Now for some fine tuning. Click Refine Effect in step 4. First we chose Subtract and a brush size of around 120 (the exact number isn't critical) and left the Opacity in the middle and painted out the areas of blur around his face. Then we switched to Add and painted back in some of the blur we lost around the front tire and behind the boy's head and off the gear levers. Little touches matter!

Now we see how he feels!

Tips on using the Speed Effect

Here are a few suggestions that may help you get the best out of this feature:

✧ Images moving sideways or up and down generally work best. You want motion that is clearly moving from one side of the frame to another, rather than towards or away from the viewer.

✧ You'll see a before and after version of the image when you're using **Guided**. You'll see the View menu at the top left. This might be particularly helpful when adding the Focus Area in step 3.

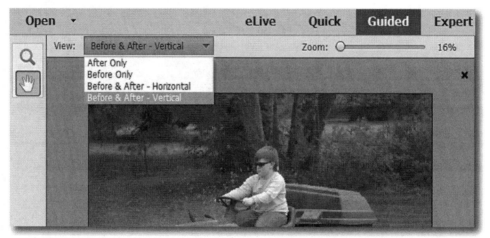

✧ Undo is available both via Edit > Undo and the keystroke CTRL-Z (Mac users: Command-Z) so if you make a change and don't like it you can always undo your last step.

✧ You *can't* move back to a previous step in the Speed Effect panel. Edit > Revert will take you back to Step 1 and undo all changes you've made and let you start over with the Speed Effect.

Tell Me More . . .

Here is a more detailed explanation of what's happening with this tool and ways you may be able to gain more control.

In Step 1, you'll use the same Quick Selection tool you'd use in the Expert editor to paint a selection. It attempts to intelligently select the area you want quickly. And, usually, it does a pretty good job! When you click Quick Selection Tool the options in Step 1 will change to allow you to control the Quick Selection Tool.

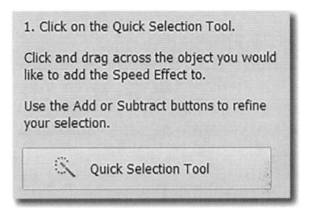

You can switch back and forth between Add and Subtract to make the adjustments you need. Adjust your brush size as needed. Click and drag to paint in the selection. Click on Subtract when you're a bit over zealous and select outside the area you want. You'll see once you do one or two of these that you don't need the selection to be perfect, but you want it to be exact.

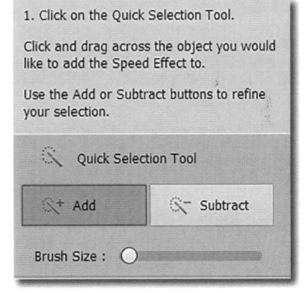

In Step 2, when you select Add Speed Effect, the right panel will change and you'll have more options.

To adjust the Speed Effect, click and drag the Angle circle to set the direction you want for the motion. This is a little tricky because the circle is very small, so it may take a few attempts.

After you set the direction, click Increase or Decrease to adjust the amount of motion blur. Clicking them repeatedly will further increase or decrease the amount of blur.

2. Click on Add Speed Effect to apply the effect.

Use the Increase or Decrease buttons to adjust the intensity of the effect.

Use the Angle control to change the angle of the effect.

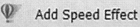 Add Speed Effect

2. Click on Add Speed Effect to apply the effect.

Use the Increase or Decrease buttons to adjust the intensity of the effect.

Use the Angle control to change the angle of the effect.

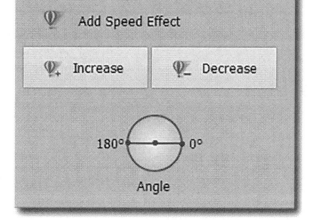

In Step 3, you'll clean up the blur to include just the areas you want. Marking these areas uses a feature we haven't seen before in Elements. You may need to practice it a bit! You're going to draw lines that mark off sections of the image that will be unaffected by the blur. To do this, click

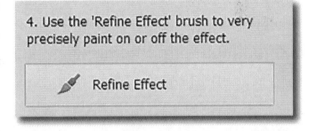

the Add Focus Area button and click and drag your cursor. You'll see the blur disappear where you draw your lines. You'll remove one strip of the blur at a time, so you'll probably need to draw a number of lines to clean it up. Don't worry about getting it too perfect—you'll refine it in Step 4.

Click Refine Effect in Step 4. Once again the panel will change and add some new controls. This is a brush tool you'll use to paint the effect to specific areas of the image.

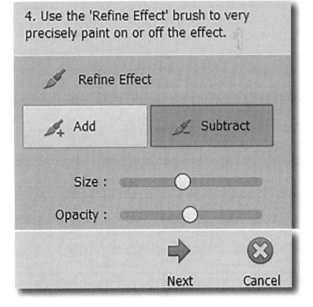

To refine the motion blur, set Size and Opacity, (how transparent you want the effect to be). Click Add to paint in the effect and click Subtract to remove areas of the effect the same way.

Finally, at the lower-right corner of the screen, click Next to continue or Cancel if you wish to return to the image and discard all the changes you've made in this **Guided** edit. Clicking Next will change the panel to allow you to choose what you do with the image now that the effect has been applied.

You can use Save or Save As (just like File > Save and File > Save As) or you can return to editing the image in the **Quick** mode or **Expert** mode. You can also Share it to various online options. Your options you see may vary from here depending on your location and any updates Adobe has made to the software.

SHAKE REDUCTION

What Does It Do?

Shake Reduction is a new feature that helps reduce blur caused by slight camera movement during the exposure. Your desired (or required) shutter speed may not always be fast enough to prevent your hand from shaking the camera slightly. Shooting while moving, such as from a car or amusement park ride can also introduce shake blur. Shake blur is different from motion blur, which is caused by the subject itself moving faster than the shutter speed of the camera is able to freeze the motion

Where Do I Find it?

Elements 14 offers two forms of this new feature: Automatic Shake Reduction and Manual Shake Reduction. You will find the Automatic version in Enhance > Auto Shake Reduction and the Manual version in Enhance > Shake Reduction.

How Do I Use it?

The Automatic version works like you'd think: automatically without any input or control from you so it's fine for a quick check to see how much it can help.

To use the Automatic version:

1. Open the image in Elements 14 (File > Open).

2. Select **Expert** at the top of the screen.

3. Use Enhance > Auto Shake Reduction.

This feature may require a few seconds or more to process the effect. During this time, your mouse pointer will turn to circling dots to indicate progress. When it's done, you'll see the results.

The Manual version is, well, more manual. To use the Manual version:

1. Open the image in Elements 14.

2. Select **Expert** at the top of the screen.

3. Choose Enhance > Shake Reduction. The Shake Reduction window will open showing your image.

4. When the Shake Reduction window opens, Elements defines a shake region with a dotted box (much like a selection marquee with a round pin in the middle) in the center of your image. The software uses this shake region as the basis for determining the kind and amount of shake it needs to correct. It then applies the correction to the entire image.

5. You can move the shake region by clicking and dragging the pin in the center. Position it where you have the kind of shake blur you'd like to reduce or remove. You can also resize the area by clicking and dragging any of the corner or side handles.

6. The Add Another Shake Region icon will let you click and drag out more shake regions if you need them.

7. If you need to see more detail, the Magnifier Window icon will display another window over the Shake Reduction results that magnify the area under it. You can click-and-drag this to move it over different areas of the image. It's like using a loupe to look closely at a particular section.

8. Adjust the Sensitivity slider for the amount of Shake Reduction. Moving to the right tends to sharpen more, to the left leaves more blur. Adjust by what looks best—there's no right or wrong here!

9. Click OK when you're done to keep your changes and close the window or Cancel to just close the window and discard your changes.

Let Me Try!

For our demonstration, we'll use Selfie from our download set, but feel free to use whatever image you like. Just make sure that the blur in the image is caused by camera shake, not motion blur (in other words the camera moved, not the subject, to create the blur).

Selfie has minor motion blur that's typical of a camera or other small phone in low light. The photographer used an average cell phone in a moving car to capture this shot. The shake blur here isn't extreme, but it could be better and really shows when we look at the girl's face (particularly her eyes) and the Great Dane's eyes and fur. The lines on the text on her t-shirt are also rather blurry where they should be crisp.

Let's try the easy way first and use Enhance > Auto Shake Reduction. Simply select the menu and see what happens!

At the left is the original image, at the right the results. It's a bit better. Her face details are more clear, the dog's eye and fur looks a bit better and the lines in the text on her shirt are a little more distinct. This will be easier to see on your screen than here in small print. Overall, not bad!

You can probably do a little better using the Manual options, though, so let's give those a try and see if we can see any real difference.

1. With the image open, choose Enhance > Shake Reduction. The Shake Reduction window appears. Note that you can move this window by clicking and dragging the title bar but you cannot resize it.

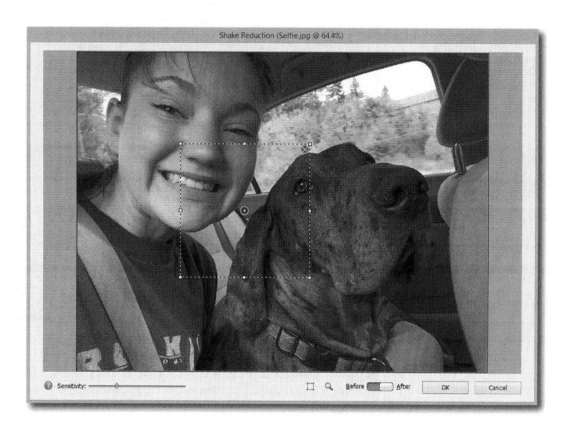

2. Move the Shake Region by clicking and dragging the dot in the middle so it's over the girl's face and includes her eyes, eyebrows and teeth. We want these to be sharp. Resize as you need to by clicking and dragging the corner or side handles on the edges of the dotted marquee.

3. We also want to make sure that the Great Dane looks as good as she can, so click Add Another Shake Region (dotted box at the bottom that looks like the Rectangular Selection Marquee tool) and a new shake region will appear. Drag it over the Dane's face and eyes and size as needed. Note the pin mark remains for the first shake region on the girl's face.

4. Adjust the Sensitivity slider to where you think it makes the best change. It doesn't make a huge difference on this image, but we liked it about three-quarters of the way over to the right.

5. Click Before/After to toggle between the original and the changed version and you'll see the changes. They're subtle, but they are there!

That's not bad! There's a lot more detail here and the image looks more crisp.

Tips on using Shake Reduction

✧ Make sure you're trying to correct camera shake, not motion blur. Motion blur is when the subjects themselves were in motion when you took the picture and that type of blurring is very different to correct because the subject will probably have differing amounts of blur than the objects in the foreground or background.

✧ Be realistic: no sharpening feature can put back detail that has been lost to extensive blur. What it can do is help make the details that *are* there more crisp and defined by enhancing their edges. But if an image is sufficiently blurred that detail is lost, neither this feature nor the sharpening features are likely to be able to do more than make what *is* in the image more distinct—not add in what wasn't captured in the first place.

✧ The larger the image you have to work with the more potential you have to make an improvement. A 3000-x-2000-pixel image is going to have a lot more detail than a 600-x-400-pixel image and more to work with in recovering and enhancing clarity. Work with the largest image you can when sharpening and clarifying!

✧ Are there alternatives to Shake Reduction? Yes. Shake Reduction is essentially a specialized version of sharpening. Unsharp Mask (Enhance > Unsharp Mask) and Adjust Sharpness (Enhance > Adjust Sharpness) are good options. Unsharp Mask is good for overall sharpening. Adjust Sharpness lets you customize the kind of blur present (motion blur, lens blur, or Gaussian (general) blur. If Shake Reduction isn't producing the results you want, these are worth trying.

✧ Using one of the other Sharpen features after applying Shake Reduction is okay! You may want to select specific areas to emphasize. Unsharp Mask and Adjust sharpness give you far more control when sharpening an image.

Tell Me More . . .

For those of you that really want to get the most out of this tool, here are a few suggestions:

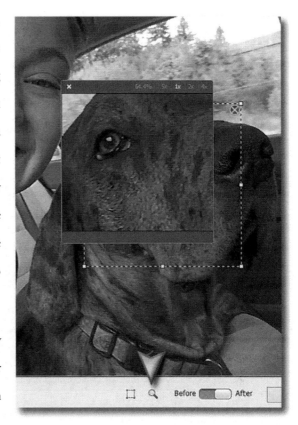

✧ It helps to zoom in and see the detail . . . but this feature lacks the usual zoom feature. The usual keystrokes for zooming won't work here, either. But you can click the Magnifying Glass icon and a Magnifier window will appear. Move it over parts of the image (click and drag by the bar at the top). You can control the amount of magnification using that same top bar. 1x = 100% zoom, 2x = 200% zoom, and so on.

✧ The magnifier window is particularly helpful when using the Sensitivity slider to see how much fine detail you can recover in various places in the image.

✧ One last trick with the Magnifier window: to close it, be sure to click the "X" in its upper-left corner. If you hit ESC (as you might be in the habit of doing when closing windows), Elements thinks you mean to click the Cancel button and will close the whole Shake Reduction window and cancel everything you've done.

✧ Within each shake region, you can also temporarily turn off that region's effect by clicking the pin in the center. It will turn dark to indicate it's inactive. Turn it back on by clicking it again.

✧ You can remove a shake region by clicking the X in the upper-right corner of the shake region.

REFINE SELECTION BRUSH ENHANCEMENTS

What Does It Do?

The Refine Selection brush lets you add or subtract from an existing selection by fine-tuning the edges. Think of it as a sophisticated version of the Quick Selection tool.

Adobe introduced the Refine Selection brush in Photoshop Elements 13 and updated it in Elements 14. It's closely related to the Select > Refine Edge feature. New features of the Refine Selection brush include the ability to soften the curvature of the edge of the selection and the ability to mask out selected areas in various ways.

Where Do I Find it?

The Refine Selection brush is the last of the four selection tools in the Select portion of the Tool box. It shares a place with the Quick Selection brush, Selection Brush, and Magic Wand. Any of those icons may be showing depending on what you last used. The Refine Selection brush will always be in the lower-right place! Click whichever is showing to be able to choose it in the Options bar.

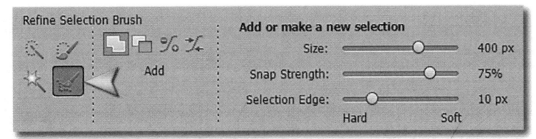

Once you've selected it in the Tool box you can choose the Refine Selection brush specifically in the Options bar by choosing it at the left. It's also the lower-right icon.

How Do I Use it?

We're going to come out and say this right up front: this one can be tricky to use and we have a bit of a love/hate relationship with the Refine selection brush. It *can* be very effective but it also can take some trial and error. And there are alternatives to using it so if you find it challenging to use, like most things in Elements, you can use other tools to refine a selection. Use whatever works best for you!

Adobe designed the Refine Selection brush to refine the edge of a selection by adding or subtracting from the selection using edge detection. Ideally, it makes complicated selections more accurate.

Before we start, let's talk about the various controls on this tool.

The Brush: The brush (your mouse cursor) for the Refine Selection brush is made up of two circles, a darker inner inner circle which indicates the size of the brush and an outer circle defining the area that will be used to look for an edge. The center of the tool also indicates whether it is adding or subtracting from the selection with a + or − mark.

The Options Bar: The options bar has many settings to define how the Refine Selection brush works.

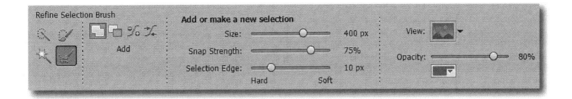

✧ At the far left, choose which selection brush to use. There are four and the Refine Selection brush is the lower-right icon.

✧ The next selection defines the mode of how the brush works. The first and second icons are the familiar Add To and Subtract From selection options and they work as you'd expect: they'll tell the brush to add to or subtract from the existing selection. The third and fourth icons are Push and Smooth.

     o **Push.** Placing the cursor inside your selection expands the selection inside the outer circle of the cursor to the nearest edge it finds. Placing the cursor outside the selection shrinks the selection within the outer circle of the cursor to the nearest edge it finds. The sensitivity of the edge detection is set in the Snap Strength slider (see below).

     o **Smooth.** Smooth smooths out the edge of the selection.

✧ The third section has three sliders that determine characteristics of the brush.

     o **Size** defines the size of the brush stroke in pixels. This is the dark inner section of the cursor. Set this the slider or by clicking the number and typing in the size.

     o **Snap Strength** sets how quickly the brush will snap to an edge when it finds one. The higher the value the quicker it will snap.

     o **Selection Edge** sets how large the selection radius is. A high value will result in gentle curves on the edge of the selection. A low value will let the edge be relatively more jagged or angular.

✧ The View section of the Options bar controls the overlay to show masking while selecting. Click the menu to choose from these options:

o **Overlay** gives you a mask effect. Unselected areas will have a masking color placed over them much like the regular Selection Brush when the mode is set to Mask. You can set the color of the overlay below the Opacity slider.

o **On Black** or **On White** set the unselected areas to solid black and white.

o **Opacity** sets how solid or transparent the mask will be, letting the image behind show through.

With all that in mind, here are the general steps to using the Refine Selection tool:

1. This feature works in either **Quick** or **Expert** mode. With one of those modes chosen, open your image.

2. Use whichever selection tool or combination of selection tools you prefer to roughly select your subject. You'll want to get it reasonably close but, of course, the Refine Selection brush is going to do the detail work.

3. Choose the Refine Selection brush by choosing the Selection Brush area in the Tool Box and then the Refine Selection brush specifically in the Options bar.

4. Select the Add To mode from the second section of the Options bar.

5. Click and drag the cursor with the dark inner portion of the pointer inside your selection and the lighter part outside it on areas where you need to add to the selection. As you click and hold it will expand, looking for the outer edge. Continue around the selection filling in all the missing places. Adjust the size as needed.

6. If you have sections that are overselected, choose the Subtract from Selection option and in the same manner, place the dark inner circle outside the selection and the lighter outer circle over the selection to remove areas of overselection.

7. Push can be used to both add to and subtract from the selection depending where you start. It will push the selection in or out.

8. Repeat steps 4 through 7 as needed to get the outline selected.

9. Finally, use the Smooth option to paint around the edge of the selection to smooth it out if needed.

Got all that? Don't worry if not—we'll walk through an example in the Let Me Try section. This is probably the most complicated selection tool and it will take some practice to master!

Let Me Try!

Let's use Balance to demonstrate the Refine Selection brush. Feel free to use your own image if you prefer.

1. Select **Expert** (or **Quick**) from the main Elements menu and use File > Open to open Balance.

2. Use the Quick Selection tool with the mode in the Options bar set to New or Add, and select the rocks and post. This doesn't have to be perfect, but don't miss the areas in shadow. Use Subtract if you need to remove large area from your selection.

3. Choose the Refine Selection tool. You want to confirm that you have everything selected, you'll want to take a close look. Make these settings in the Options bar:

    a. Select Add in the Options bar

    b. Set View to Overlay

    c. Set Opacity to 80%

    d. Set Color to Red

4. You should now see the area outside the selection in red with the background image faintly showing through.

5. Zoom in to 100% to see where you may be missing areas. Use View > Actual Pixels, any of the other view options you prefer, or CTRL + or - (Mac users: command + or -) to zoom in and out. Now you can see areas missed in the selection that weren't easily visible when the image was full size.

6. Set the Size of the brush to 120 px (pixels), leave Snap Strength at 75% and since these are nice round shapes, choose a Selection Edge about midway on the slider of 5 px.

7. Move the cursor so the dark portion is *inside* the selected area while the lighter outer area of the cursor covers the *unselected* area. Click, hold, and gently move the cursor around and the selection will fill in. Repeat as needed.

8. To remove unwanted areas that are selected, such as the space between the rocks, set the mode to Subtract. Experiment a little here! We found this worked well with the Size of the brush set to 30 px, Snap Strength at 75%, and Selection Edge reduced to 2 px because the angles between the rocks are pretty sharp—we don't want rounded edges there.

9. Consider using the Push option to push selections either direction.

10. When you're done, use the Smooth mode if you need to to polish any rough areas.

Finally, to remove the mask, choose one of the other tools (such as the Quick Selection tool) and the mask will return to the more familiar marquee (marching ants).

What do you do with it now? That's up to you. Here's one idea for using a selection like this.

- With the rocks selected, use Enhance > Adjust Lighting > Contrast/Brightness and increase Contrast to +30.

- Use Select > Inverse to select the background instead of the rocks and then adjust the color with Enhance > Adjust Color > Adjust Hue/Saturation and set Saturation to -100 (to remove all color) and Lightness to -40 to darken it a bit.

- Add the text using the Horizontal Type tool. The color for the text at the top came from the middle rock and the color for the text at the bottom came from the fourth rock. The Effects on *FOCUS* are 42 pt Bevel, Up, and a 13 pt Stroke, Black, positioned Outside.

Tips on Using the Refine Selection Brush

Here are some suggestions to making a detailed refined selection on a complex subject:

- Don't hesitate to use a variety of selection tools if one will work better than another for selecting a particular area. Specifically:

  a. The Polygonal Lasso is excellent for selecting straight areas.

  b. The Lasso is very handy for selecting odd-shaped areas or quickly selecting loose sections.

  c. The Quick Selection tool is great if there is a clear difference between what you want selected and not. It won't work well with close colors or areas where there isn't a clear transition.

  d. The Magic Wand is ideal for selecting areas of similar color, such as sky.

- Zoom in! It's very hard to see details if you're zoomed out. It's also very hard to be precise with the mouse if the image is small.

- The bracket keys ([and]) can be used any time to change the size of your brush. This is much easier than moving your cursor down to the Options bar.

- Change the size of your brush when you need to. A small brush can't easily paint a large area and a large brush won't get small details.

- Hold the Space bar down to get the hand tool at any time so you can click, drag, and scroll through the image without having to use the scroll bars. This is really helpful when zoomed in.

✧ Use Select > Save Selection after you complete a complicated selection so you can bring it back if you accidentally deselect your image or want to work with that selection in a later session.

✧ Take it slow. The selection will fill in more as you click and hold so don't move too quickly.

✧ Work in short sections. It's tempting to select the entire object at once, but it's a lot easier if you do it in short sections if you make a mistake—you only have to undo that last little bit.

Tell Me More . . .

Need more control than the Refine Selection brush? The Refine Edge feature is still in Elements 14 (Select > Refine Edge). With Refine Edge you can also add and subtract from an existing selection using edge detection but it also allows you to adjust the overall edge by smoothing, feathering, changing contrast, or shifting the edge. You then choose what to create with the results: a selection mask, layer, or new document. This isn't a new feature to Elements 14 so we won't cover it in detail here, but if you're not familiar with it (or have forgotten about it!) it's a useful tool for detail work.

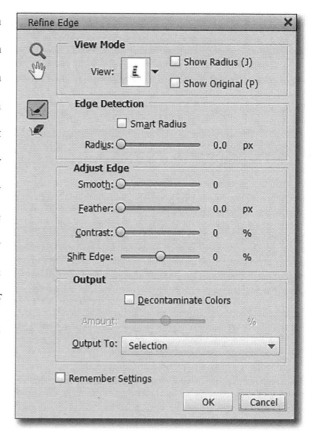

SMART LOOKS EFFECT

What Does It Do?

Smart Looks automatically suggests five different looks for your image based on the color and lighting within the image, giving each a different style or feeling that Adobe hopes enhances the strengths of the image. If you're looking for ideas for what to do with an image creatively, Smart Looks can quickly show you some different options tailored specifically to the makeup of each specific photo.

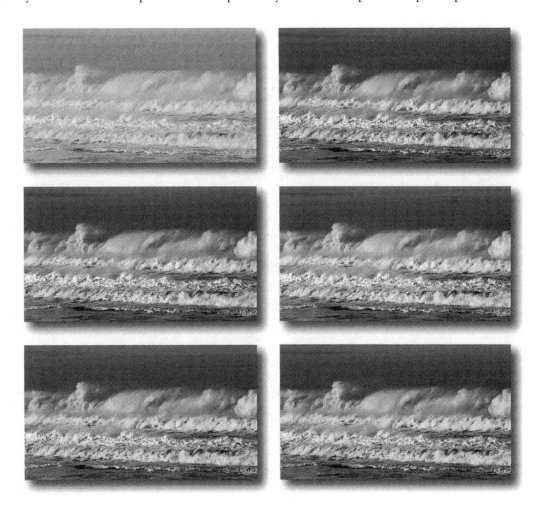

Where Do I Find it?

Smart Looks is part of Quick Effects panel. Choose the **Quick** mode at the top of the screen and then click the Effects icon in the lower-right corner

just below the panel. The panel on the right will show all the available Effects. Smart Looks will be at the top of the panel. You may need to click the arrow to open that section of the panel if you only see one thumbnail instead of the full five. You'll see the arrow after hovering your mouse cursor over the Smart Looks thumbnail.

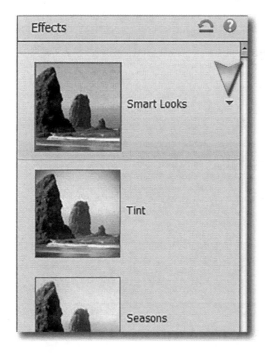

How Do I Use it?

Smart Looks is pretty easy to use. The real trick is just knowing that it's there and where it is. Frankly we don't spend a lot of time in **Quick** and could easily have overlooked this new feature but we think it's pretty handy for a quick way to find a new look for an image.

Follow these steps to use Smart Looks:

1. Open the image you wish to use.

2. Select **Quick** if you're not already there, then choose the Effects panel in the lower-right corner.

3. If you don't see five Smart Looks thumbnails, hover the mouse cursor over the Smart Looks section in the panel at right and click the arrow to open the Smart Looks. You'll see thumbnails of five different looks for your image.

4. Click any of the five effects you see. Your image will immediately change based on what you've chosen. You can change as often as you like between the different options.

If you want to keep the change, you don't need to do anything else (there is no Done button or checkmark). If you wish to reset the image back to the original, click the Reset icon at the top of the Effects panel. You can also use Edit > Revert.

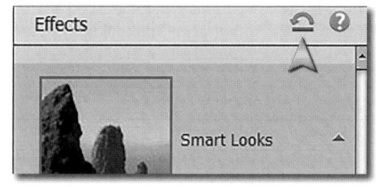

Let Me Try!

We'll use the Ocean image from the download set, but feel free to use this or your own image if you prefer.

This image of a stormy day on the Oregon Coast has a lot of potential drama but it's a little flat when it comes to tone and color. It lacks punch. Let's see what Elements 14 can do with the Smart Looks effect in **Quick**.

1. Open the Ocean Image (File > Open).

2. Choose **Quick** at the top of the screen, then the Effects panel at the lower-right corner.

3. If you need to, open the Smart Looks effect by clicking the arrow by the Smart Looks thumbnail. You won't see the arrow until the mouse cursor is moved over the thumbnail.

4. You'll see the five different looks the Smart Looks effect suggests for the image. Here are the results, including the original image first:

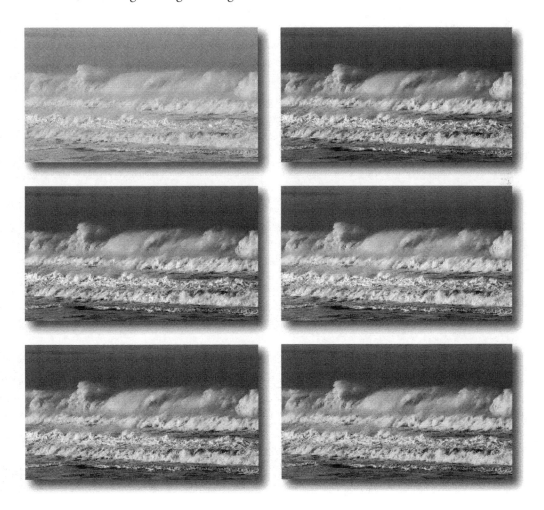

Each has its own appeal! One thing is consistent: there is a lot more contrast in the Smart Looks suggestions, which isn't surprising. The original image is a bit washed out. Now we have five different looks that fix that problem.

Tips on using the Smart Looks effect

Here are some suggestions for working with Smart Looks:

✧ These are Quick Edits and that means you don't have any control over how they work. Elements makes changes based on the color and lighting automatically and you can't change that here. If you want more control, edit the images manually in Expert and use the editing features there. Of course, you can start with the results from Smart Looks, switch to Expert, and take it from there.

✧ Remember that in Quick mode you have a View option in the upper-left corner of the screen to show you before, after, and a combined view, horizontally or

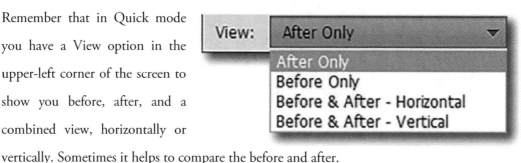

vertically. Sometimes it helps to compare the before and after.

✧ Although they're not new, there are quite a few other options for quick effects in Smart Looks. Consider these if you're trying to give an image a different look.

Tell Me More . . .

You may be wondering just how the image was changed in each case. While specifics aren't available or selectable, we can take a good guess. A great tool for evaluating an image is always the histogram. You can see the histogram for each image by making the change in Quick edit and then switching to Expert and choosing Window > Histogram. Let's take a look at each of these and see what we can learn.

Learning to interpret a histogram can really help improve your editing and choosing how you want to achieve a desired effect.

The above image is the original with original histogram. As you can see it's rather heavily shifted towards the right, indicating mostly lighter tones and not much in the shadows and blacks (which would show up in the far left). That's not surprising given our subject but a few more tones in those areas would significantly increase contrast.

This is the first option. The histogram shows us a couple of things: first that it's more balanced overall and shifted to the left, increasing the darker tones. And, second, that the colors are more balanced across the range. When you balance colors, you tend to get a grayer look (three identical intensities of red, green, and blue give you a shade of gray). So, here we get an image with more contrast and less color, but definitely more impact!

In the second option the tones are more spread out giving more blacks and shadows (and thus better contrast), but the colors aren't so equalized so we have bright blues instead of a lot of gray. We get a very contrasty, colorful image.

This fourth image blends the second and third--more contrast and some color, but neither as bright nor as subdued.

This last image has a sepia or old-fashioned look (can't you just see an old pirate ship sailing along behind it?) with more earth tones and not nearly as much strength in the blues.

Editing using Levels (Enhance > Adjust Lighting > Levels) is the main way to control the distribution of tones in an image. By default, Levels has the Channels menu set to RGB, meaning it adjusts the Red, Green and Blue channels all at once the same way. You may find it more effective to choose each channel individually in the Levels window, adjust that channel, then proceed to the next channel. That can let you emphasize blues, for example, more than reds or greens.

Are you wondering why the histograms are jagged in the edited versions? We refer to that effect *combing* (as in a hair comb). It happens when the histogram stretches a narrow range of tones out over a wider range—and gaps in the histogram develop. With a JPEG image there are 256 tones for each channel of Red, Green, and Blue (8 bits per channel). If you try to stretch a range of 10 tones across 20, there will be some gaps. It's also a contributor to why some images can look a little grainy when heavily processed: there isn't enough color information to spread the colors out over a range.

This is one reason why a camera raw file (which has more information per pixel for color than a JPEG) can sometimes produce superior quality results when improving exposure-type issues. A raw file may have as many as 16 bits per channel, or more than 65,000 shades to work with. That's a lot more to work with when spreading out a narrow range.

PHOTOMERGE® CHANGES

What Does It Do?

Photomerge® combines several images into one (either horizontally or vertically). Previous versions of Photoshop Elements included the Photomerge® tools and they're still there, but in Elements 14, you now have a user-friendly interface with step-by-step instructions.

As of Elements 13 (and still in Elements 14), the six Photomerge® tools are:

✧ **Compose**, which lets you merge a portion of one image into another.

✧ **Exposure**, which allows you to combine the dynamic range of multiple exposures of the same shot into a single shot like High Definition Range (HDR) processing.

✧ **Faces**, which helps you combine multiple facial features from different photos into a single image.

✧ **Group Shot**, which assists you in creating a group shot from subjects in multiple photos.

✧ **Panorama**, which lets you stitch together multiple images into a single very wide (or tall) panoramic image.

✧ **Scene Cleaner**, which provides you with a helpful tool for removing unwanted elements in your image by merging in areas from similar pictures

Where Do I Find it?

You'll find the set of Photomerge® features in **Guided**. Choose **Guided** at the top of the screen, then choose Photomerge® at the right in the bar just below to see the six options.

Like all the **Guided** features, you'll have a large thumbnail and brief explanation of each of the Photomerge® options. Move your mouse across each thumbnail to see before-and-after examples for each effect. It's easier than remembering what each one does just by name!

How Do I Use it?

To use any of the Photomerge® options:

1. Open the images you want to use

2. Choose **Guided**

3. Choose Photomerge®

4. Select a specific Photomerge® effect

If you don't open the images needed for the Photomerge® effect first, a box will appear letting you know how many you need. It will then return to Photomerge® **Guided** edit where you can open the images. You may also need to select your images by CTRL-clicking (Mac users: Command-clicking) in the Photo Bin at the bottom of your screen, as in the case of the alert shown to the right.

After that, it's just a matter of following the step-by-step instructions on your screen.

Let Me Try!

With one exception, these features haven't changed from the previous version. They look a bit different and have more detailed instructions but in most cases the process remains the same, so we won't walk through each one in detail. Instead, we'll highlight the differences you'll need to know as you get used to Elements 14.

Five of the six Photomerge° options, Compose, Exposure, Faces, Group Shot, and Scene Cleaner remain virtually identical to previous versions. After you're done, however, you'll have the option to Save, Continue Editing, or Share your new image, much like other Guided Edits.

Photomerge° looks a little different, however, but fortunately Adobe has rearranged the features, not changed them. Since the functionality is consistent, we'll just discuss they key things you need to know:

✧ Be sure to select the images you want included in the panorama *prior* to choosing Photomerge® Panorama.

✧ You'll find the former Layout options in a menu in the Panorama Settings section at the right. Click the menu to choose a layout.

✧ If you don't see the settings, click the triangle next to Settings and you'll have the familiar Blend Images Together, Vignette Removal, and Geometric Distortion Correction options again.

✧ Click Create Panorama at the bottom right to merge the images. This may take a few seconds, depending on the size, number, and complexity of the images.

✧ When Photomerge° completes the process, it will return to Expert mode and usually ask you if you'd like Elements to fill in or clean the edges. Depending on the image this can be very effective, or not. It's worth trying,

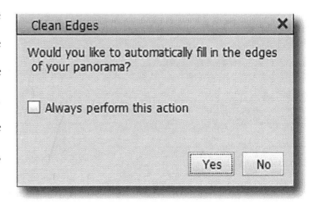

though, as it may save you some time and reduce the amount you'll need to crop away.

✧ After the option to Clean Edges, Elements will return to the familiar Guided Edit screen to save, edit, or share your image.

Tips on Using the Photomerge®Features

With Guided Edit, it's easy to follow the step-by-step instructions at the side of the screen. Follow each step!

Tell Me More . . .

We use Photomerge° Panorama most frequently and really like the way it works. While the basic functionality hasn't changed, here are a few suggestions for getting the best results from Photomerge° Panorama.

- ✦ Use large images. If you resize your images before using Panorama, Elements may have difficulty matching up the edges. Where possible use the original size images. If you're having trouble with computer memory issues or a very slow response time, you may need to resize your images to a smaller size before you begin. (Use File > Process Multiple Images to resize a batch of images in Photoshop Elements.)

- ✦ Experiment with different choices in the Panorama Settings option (Auto, Perspective, Cylindrical, and so on). Sometimes one will produce a more pleasing result with your particular set of images.

- ✦ Shoot with panoramic images in mind: shooting the images at the same level, including a fair amount of overlap between the images, and trying to keep the exposures similar.

- ✦ We've found the Clean Edge option works in some situations and not others. It's worth trying, but you may need to do some additional clean up.

- ✦ In previous versions of Elements you had a Browse feature to search for unopened images to add to Photomerge°. That no longer exists, so open all the images you want to merge first.

ELEMENTS 14 ORGANIZER

If you've taken our online classes in Elements, you'll know we spend the majority of our time there on the Editor and we've placed the same priorities in this book. Elements Organizer gives you a number of organizational tools, although we find that Adobe Lightroom is a far more sophisticated product and both of us greatly prefer Lightroom for organization.

Organizer has several ways of organizing photos based on faces, places, and date and time. That's where you'll see the majority of updates in Elements 14. If you're using Organizer already, these will be easy to use and we won't spend too much time here on them, as they're mostly enhancements rather than extensive new features or functionality. If you haven't used Organizer, you may want to start with the Adobe tutorials on that so you can fully appreciate the options Adobe offers.

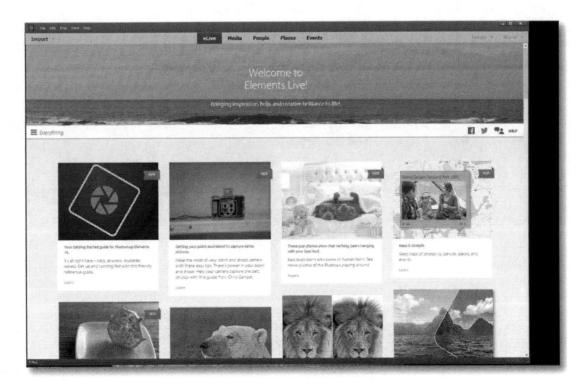

People Recognition

While Organizer has a long history of recognizing people in your pictures, with version 14 there are some new enhancements. You'll see some advanced grouping and easier ways to select the faces you want and use batch processing to get the job done quickly. If you are tagging people, you can easily combine this with identified people.

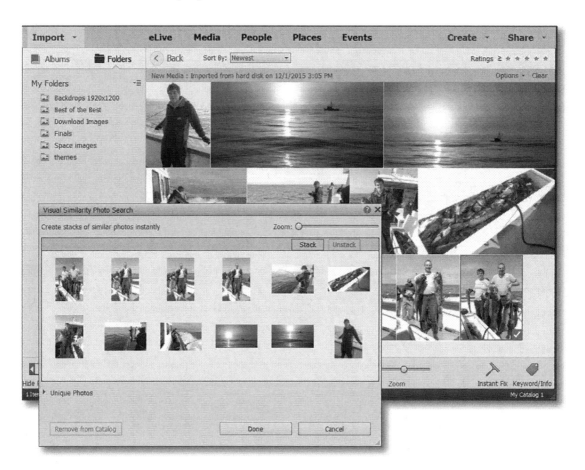

Date and Time

Again, Adobe has enhanced the ways you can search and organize based on date and time of your photos. This is especially handy if you're looking for a specific event or trip and can connect it to a particular period of time. You'll find new tools to help you gather images together quickly, use tagging, and organize them the way that makes sense to you.

For example, if you choose the Event view, you can see images grouped together by various date groupings.

Places

Using the mapping features of Organizer lets you visually organize your work, especially those media files with GPS information. And, with Elements 14 you'll find an improved interface to speed up your search and locate operations. Personalized locations and custom names give you the flexibility you want. Use the Places tab to help locate your images to particular locations.

Importing

If you've been using Organizer, you'll understand about importing files to the Organizer, where files are not stored, but simply catalogued. With Elements 14, Adobe has streamlined this process to get you going on your projects faster than ever! Working in batches (by choosing Import > In Bulk) is one of the ways Adobe has updated Elements 14 and if you're using Organizer for all your images, this is a key feature.

If you want to import images from many sources, click Add Folder in the lower-left corner and select as many folders as you'd like.

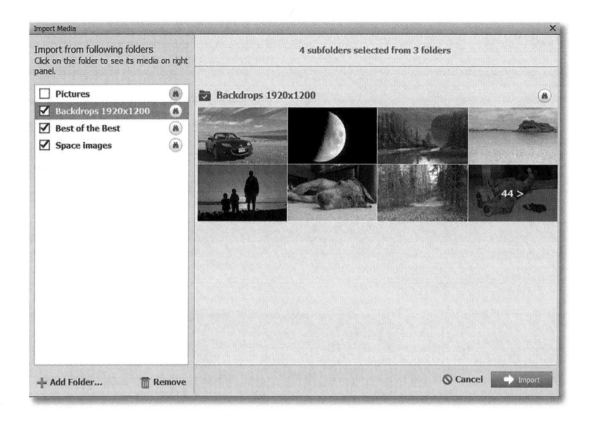

Adobe's website also tells us that, "Elements Organizer includes more enhancements such as performance improvements, support for European date format, ability to create a video story from within Organizer and various bug fixes."

If you're currently using Organizer and want to explore the new updates, you'll find them ready and waiting for you. In the Adobe Help pages, you'll find tutorials if you need more help or want to start from scratch in understanding the options of Organizer.

TIDBITS

Adobe created a few more changes in Elements 14 we don't want to overlook! In this section, we'll discuss:

- ✦ More details about the Organizer catalog message and saving files

- ✦ A new look in Guided Edit

- ✦ A before-and-after preview feature for each Guided Edit

- ✦ Changes to Preferences

- ✦ An improved (and much easier) way to reset Preferences

- ✦ File Info feature and metadata

Details on Organizer Catalog Message and Saving Files

When you first start using Elements 14 and save your work you may be presented with a message about organizing and needing to create a catalog.

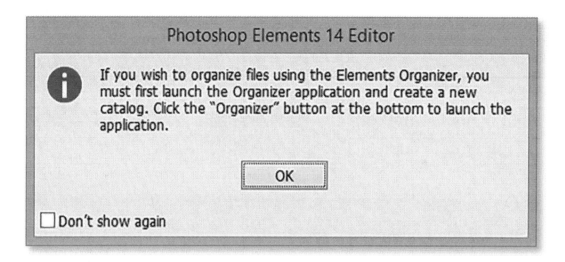

This isn't a problem--it's just letting you know that at present you haven't created a catalog for Organizer to use to manage your images. Once you've launched Organizer you'll have a catalog and this message won't appear. However, until you create a catalog, when saving a file you will not be able to check the Include in the Elements Organizer box to automatically include that image in your Organizer catalog.

In the following image of the lower portion of a Save As dialog box you'll see the difference between having a catalog in Organizer and not. In the top version, you haven't created an Organizer catalog so Include in the Elements Organizer is grayed out and unavailable. In the second image, a catalog does exist, so Include in the Elements Organizer checkbox is available.

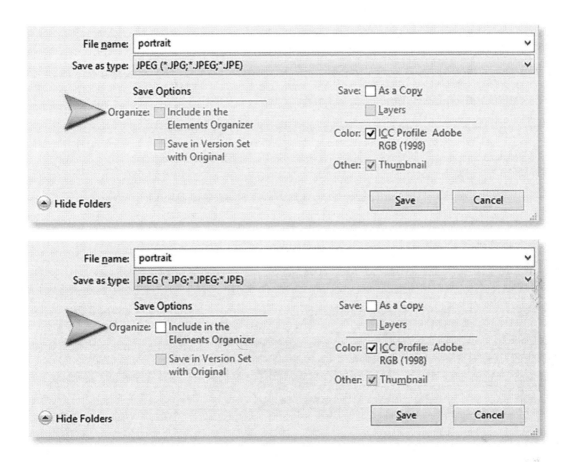

If you do come across this message and do want your image included in an Organizer catalog, cancel the Save and launch Organizer to set up your catalog. Then you can return to the Elements Editor and save the file and include it in your newly created catalog.

Guided Edit Redesign

If you've reviewed the Speed Effect or Photomerge® sections of this book, you've probably noticed that Guided Edit has a new look. In the past you might have overlooked Guided Edit, but spend a little time there and you'll find some important tools and help for interesting effects.

If you're new to Guided Edit, it contains wizard-like tools to help you achieve a particular effect with step-by-step directions. This simplifies complex editing and can be a lot of fun!

To start using Guided Edit, click the **Guided** button at the top center of the screen.

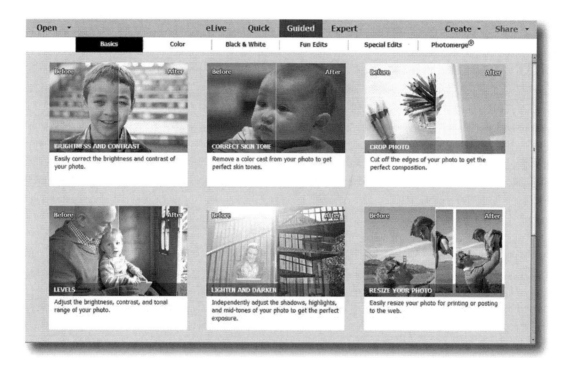

The ribbon (or menu across the top of the screen) allows you to choose from a number of different project types.

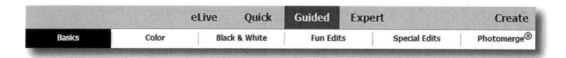

You'll find:

- ✧ **Basics.** These are among the most common changes and they'll sound familiar: Brightness and Contrast, Correct Skin Tone, Crop Photo, Levels, Lighten and Darken, Resize, Rotate and Straighten, Sharpen, and Vignette Effect.

- ✧ **Color.** You'll find help here for color issues with Enhance Color, Lomo Camera Effect, Remove Color Cast, and Saturated Film Effect.

- ✧ **Black and White.** For an emphasis on contrast and detail with a nostalgic, classical look, you might prefer black-and-white options like: Black and White, B&W Color Pop, B&W Selection, High Key, Line Drawing, and Low Key.

- ✧ **Fun Edits.** Want to get creative or need an idea for an image? Try these! Old Fashioned Photo, Out of Bounds, Picture Stack, Pop Art, Puzzle Effect, Reflection, Speed Effect, and Zoom Burst effect.

- ✧ **Special Edits.** These provide more complex improvements to your images: Depth of Field, Orton Effect, Perfect Portrait, Recompose, Restore Old Photo, Scratches and Blemishes, and Tilt-Shift.

- ✧ **Photomerge®.** This is a family of tools to help combine multiple images into one, including Compose, Exposure, Faces, Group Shot, Scene Cleaner, and of course, Panorama. We covered this in detail in the Photomerge® section of this book,

Guided Edit Previews

Instead of a generic icon, you now have a live preview for each Guided Edit. A large thumbnail lets you see a before-and-after view. Drag your mouse across each thumbnail to see the effect. This is fun but also functional. You get a better idea of exactly what the effect does and if it will be a good choice for what you want. You'll also find a description of what each Guided option does.

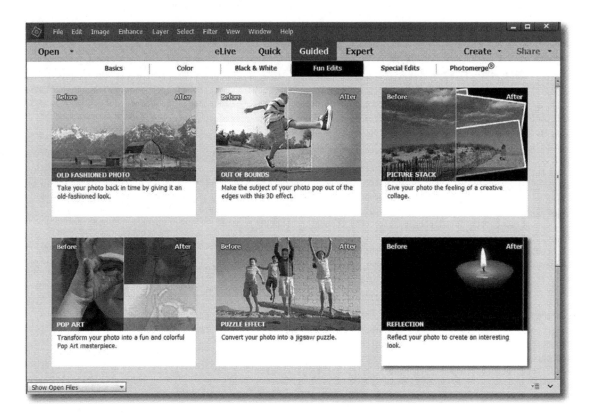

Changes to Preferences

Photoshop Elements lets you customize many of the settings and options it uses via the **Preferences** dialog. Preferences can be viewed by choosing Edit > Preferences (Mac users: Photoshop Elements > Preferences).

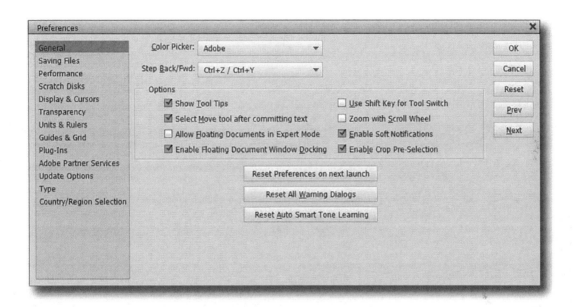

Changes to the Elements 14 Preferences include:

✧ **Scratch Disks.** Scratch Disks is a feature that allows Elements to use hard-drive storage if it's running out of memory on your computer while performing an operation. Formerly located under the Performance section in Preferences, Adobe moved Scratch Disks to its own category on the left menu.

✧ **Update Options.** Application Updates has been renamed and is now referred to as Update Options. You control whether to automatically download updates to Elements or to receive an alert when one is available.

✧ **Country and Region.** You can now select preferences by country. When you install Elements you choose a country or region. That affects which options are available such as print services or metric versus US Customary measurements, based on what's appropriate to your location. Now you can change that preference instead of having to reinstall the software if you take your computer to a new country or region.

Resetting Preferences

One more feature we want to highlight, (and we admit, it's not new to version 14, but it was to version 13!) is resetting Preferences. So, just in case you missed it, let's take a look at the ability to reset the Preferences. Easily. And that's a big deal.

Elements stores Preference information in a file. Elements relies on this file to remember all your preferences and previous settings. It's everything you've done and chosen to customize in Elements. Since we use this file a lot, it may get damaged or corrupted. The damaged file generates all sorts of odd things in the software functions. We've seen it happen many, many times with our students and ourselves. Menus will go gray, controls disappear, operations don't complete or do what they're not supposed to… and quite often you can fix these types of problems by simply resetting Preferences.

Up through version 12, you reset preferences using a bit of keyboard gymnastics and near-perfect timing: holding down ALT-CTRL-SHIFT (Mac: Option-Command-SHIFT) while Elements was loading and not before it got started. That required split second timing before Elements loaded (who would have thought there was an advantage to slower computers!)

Version 13 improved that. In Preferences > General you'll now find a button to reset the Preferences the next time you launch Photoshop Elements.

1. Click the button **Reset Preferences on next launch**
2. Close Photoshop Elements
3. Restart Photoshop Elements

You no longer need Bach-like keyboard skills to reset things.

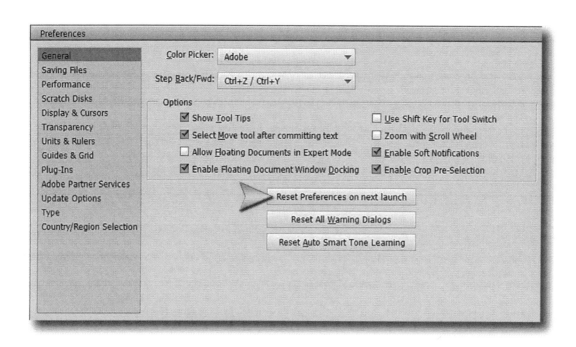

Changes to File Info

File info (File > File Info) gives you a great deal of information about an image. It's actually stored in the image file as metadata (information about the file itself, or sometimes referred to as data about data). The File Info window shows you information about the camera used, copyright, author, and caption, as well as many other details. It also lets you add and modify this information.

In Elements 14, the design of this window has changed. Previously, each major topic had a tab across the top of the screen, but the number of tabs didn't fit, so the tabs scrolled across the top which was a little awkward. Now you choose the topics from a panel at the left and the information on that topic displays at the right, much more like we see in Preferences.

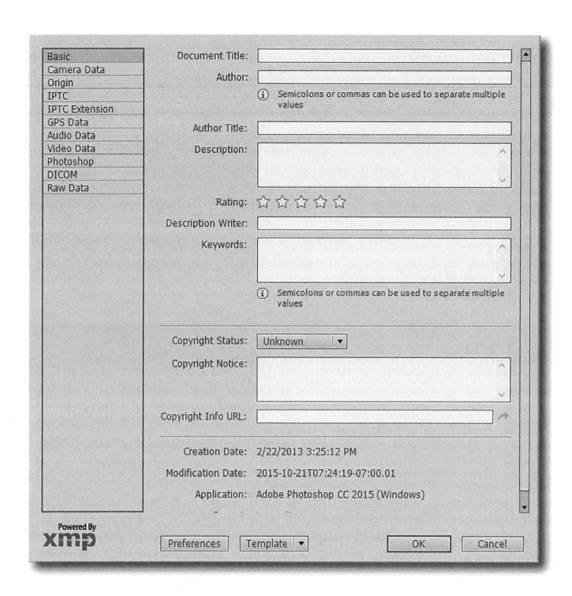

It's primarily a change in layout, but it makes working with this dialog easier. If you use and refer to metadata for your images, this will help.

THE COVER IMAGE

How did you create the ocelot image on the cover?

Our cover image showcases a few of Elements 14's new features, in particular Haze Removal, the Refine Selection options, the Out of Bounds Guided Edit. We'll leave the exact details, as they say in old college textbooks, "as an exercise for the student", but we thought you might be interested in our general workflow. There are no doubt many different ways to go about making this image but hopefully this'll give you a few ideas to get you started. Make it your own way!

Noise

The photographer (Mickela Schulz) shot the original through glass and that resulted in some shadows and subtle noise. It's a great image and we really wanted it to pop for the cover, so we planned to enhance the contrast. But, when you enhance contrast you emphasize differences. So before we worked with contrast, we reduced noise to smooth out any differences.

First we selected the eyes, inverted the selection (Select > Inverse) so everything but the eyes were selected, and used the Filter > Noise > Reduce Noise filter to reduce some of the noise. It wasn't perfect but it helped. Noise reduction can soften things a bit and we didn't want that to happen to the eyes so we excluded them from the selection. Reducing noise is always a bit of a tradeoff!

Other ideas: using the Blur filters can help so long as they don't take out too much detail. In particular Filter > Blur > Smart Blur and Filter > Blur > Surface Blur may be helpful for these sorts of situations as they offer the most control.

Duplicate Copy

At this point, we made a duplicate layer of the Background image (Layer > Duplicate Layer). We'll use this later to show the shift from original to fully edited. After you duplicate it, turn the duplicate layer off using the "eye" icon so it's not interfering anywhere. We'll come back to it later.

Dehazing

This was probably the simplest part. Enhance > Haze Removal and we adjusted the sliders to our liking. That's it!

Pre-selecting

If you're familiar with the Out of Bounds Guided feature, it includes a selection tool and will deselect any active selections you have when you start it. However, the tool in the Out of Bounds Guided feature is basically the Quick Selection tool and it's fine for the basics, but this was, frankly, a tough selection with the hair and in particular the whiskers. We needed to use a number of selection features that just aren't in the guided edit. But, this feature can use Select > Load Selection, so we *can* make our detailed selection in advance. This took a long time and a lot of trial and error so don't expect to get this right the first try.

One thing we quickly learned after we started selecting was that we needed to know just how much of this image needed to be selected. We wanted the impression of the head coming out of the frame – but just that, so that defined what we selected. No point in being super detailed about a section you're not going to need selected!

Once that was decided, here are the tools we used:

- ✧ **Quick Selection** to get the majority selected. Add and Subtract from Selection were helpful in getting the rougher areas defined. Zooming in a lot helped as did changing brush sizes depending on what we needed to select. Don't try to select the whiskers this way – there are better ways.

- ✧ **Magic Wand** to get the whiskers. With a tolerance set to between 10 and 20 and using Add to Selection we selected as much of the whiskers as we reasonably could.

- ✧ **Magnetic Lasso** to fix the whiskers. By clicking frequently to set anchoring points we were able to roughly select the tougher parts of the whiskers.

- ✧ **Select > Refine Selection** was used to smooth out the selection and make sure it wasn't capturing any of the background which would really stand out. The Refine Selection would also be a good choice here.

- ✧ **Select > Save Selection** was used frequently to frequently save this complex selection so we didn't have to reselect. We also selected in small areas at a time so Edit > Undo would work well for us and we wouldn't have to backtrack quite as far when the inevitable mis-selection happened.

Out of Bounds Effect

The Out of Bounds effect is under **Guided** in the Fun Edits section. It's a little tricky to use at first. Step one has you define the shape of the frame so draw it around where you want the frame to be. As the instructions state you can also give the frame some skew to give it a sense of perspective and we did.

After you've defined the size, location, and shape of your frame, you'll need to select your subject. We used Select > Load Selection and reloaded our detailed selection. Simpler subjects may work fine with just the Selection Tool in the right hand panel, but not this one.

When you're all selected, click the Out of Bounds effect. Here's where you'll find if your selection was accurate or not. Ours wasn't (those whiskers are *challenging* to select) and we clicked Cancel and went back to our image, loaded the selection, adjusted it, and went through this process several times before we got what we wanted. If you finally do, you'll have our ocelot peeking out of the frame and the whiskers nicely defined.

All that's left to do is click Add Background Gradient to fill in the background and you have the usual range of gradient-type fill options here.

Finally, choose which size shadow you want to use. These are basically drop shadows to help the image stand out against the frame and it's an effective way to do that. The small or medium looked best to us, but depending on your image and preferences, use whatever works best for you!

Click Next and then back to the Editor for more work.

Gradient Mask

If you look closely you'll notice that our ocelot on the cover starts at the left in the hazy version and by the time of his head he's had all the haze removed but it's a gradual change. This is a layer mask using a gradient and is where our duplicate layer comes in handy. What we want is a mask (a covering that lets you see through) show in a graduated way across the image.

First we moved our duplicate layer to the top of the layer stack in the Layers panel.

Next we used the Polygonal lasso tool to select the inside of the image (inside the frame). This left part of the head outside the image and that's ok.

We inverted the selection (Select > Inverse) and then deleted away everything outside the image by pressing Delete on the keyboard. Now we have a layer that has the original version of the image inside the frame. And it looks like we lost all our good work but we haven't.

With that duplicate layer selected, we clicked the Add Layer Mask button. Then we chose the Gradient tool, picked a black-to-white pattern and clicked and dragged out a gradient over the ocelot, starting about the left-most eye and dragging about half-way across the ocelot. Viola, a mask with the gradient is applied and we have now blended the duplicate layer with all the other layers.

Final Touches

Finally, we used the Sponge tool set to saturate and lightly emphasized the contrast on the face and a little of the body. This is a good time for a bit of spot sharpening as well.

You'll probably end up with about nine layers doing this. Yes, it's a bit complicated, but this is a sophisticated image. If you want to change any of the other layers, such as the gradient, frame, etc., you can do that now!

Hope you enjoyed this little side-trip.

My Notes

My Notes

My Notes

My Notes

My Notes

My Notes

ABOUT THE AUTHORS

Beverly Richards Schulz is a graduate of the New York Institute of Photography and teaches photography through Ed2Go.com. She's also adjunct faculty for the University of San Francisco in Visual Arts, travels and exhibits her work in a variety of venues and galleries, and volunteers with the Hands Legacy Project making photographic memories for families in Hospice. Photoshop Elements is one of her favorite programs and she thoroughly enjoys teaching and learning with her students.

Eric Johnson holds degrees in secondary education and a Masters in Business Administration. His first career was at Microsoft in various technical support, managerial, and analytical roles. He adopted digital photography back when a 3 megapixel camera cost about $1000. He's worked with Beverly at Instructional and Photographic Services since 2004 designing digital photography, Photoshop, Photoshop Elements, and Photoshop Lightroom courses as IPS's Course Administrator. In what little spare time he has Eric enjoys outdoor photography, hiking, fishing, spending time with family, and anything that gets him near the ocean.

You can reach Beverly and Eric at www.bevschulz.com or via our Facebook page at https://www.facebook.com/DiscoverDigitalPhotography.

Made in the USA
Lexington, KY
06 March 2016